GW00832067

PATTERN BEYOND CHANCE

PATTERN BEYOND CHANCE

❄

Stephen Payne

HAPPENSTANCE

By the same author:
The Probabilities of Balance, Smiths Knoll pamphlet, 2010

First published in 2015
by HappenStance Press
21 Hatton Green, Glenrothes KY7 4SD
www.happenstancepress.com

Printed and bound in the UK by
Berforts Information Press, Stevenage

ISBN 978-1-910131-17-6

Contents

❀ MIND ❀

❀ TIME ❀

PATTERN BEYOND CHANCE

DESIGN

❉

'Everyone designs who devises courses of action aimed at changing existing situations into preferred ones.'

Simon, H. A. (1969). *The sciences of the artificial.* Cambridge, MA: MIT Press.

THE SCIENCE OF THE ARTIFICIAL

This beaten track to the river
you've so often walked
with your retriever—
is it cause or effect?

You unclip his leash and watch.
He snuffles and fusses
along a blackthorn hedge,
belly fur brushing the unruly grasses,

a bundle of reflex arcs, product
of a natural process;
also an artifact,
designed for some purpose

he's never fulfilled,
though expert at games of fetch
and giving you another mouth to feed,
another head to scratch.

MAKING A LIVING

If you want to know what it's like to be a butcher
or an accountant, a civil engineer
or a dairy farmer—ask a psychologist.

Herbert A. Simon could tell you a thing or two.
His pastime of choice on train journeys
was to enquire after a stranger's occupation,
pretend it was his own as well, and talk shop.

Let him try this one. *I stand still on a bicycle*
says the thin young man I'm sitting opposite.
He wanted to race, but was always better
at beginnings than endings.
Now he holds the world record and makes it pay.

He works at track events, balancing all day
in the dead centre of the velodrome.
Why should he care if he's a gimmick for the ads
when he draws the cyclists' respect?
He tells me he's happiest when a sprint is on,
the cheers ricocheting around the arena
leaving him alone with his concentration
and resolve, his skill for its own sake. Tougher
during breaks, when eyes turn to him
and his every sway is noticed.

I suggest The Guinness Book of Records
makes it hard to keep his feet on the ground,
and while he constructs a polite response

I see myself on a yellow racer, angling the front wheel
against its design for speed,
shifting a little weight from pedal to pedal:
now almost invisible in my stillness,
lost in the white noise of applause for others;
now the main show, jostled
by the crowd's unfathomable murmurings.

THE FRACTAL LIBRARY

He drifts in silence around the cliffs of language.
    From out here, nothing's clear
except gross shape, the landmarks and the signage

mapping the territory he would explore.
    He crosses bays, makes forays
down channels for a place to come ashore.

He stands at the rock face, cranes his neck to scan
    the ink-black nooks and cracks,
to plot a course of step and grasp, to plan

his zigzag ascent. The closer he looks
    the deeper he can see
the way a book makes room for further books

between its lines. He reaches for a ledge:
    How strong his hold? How long
this coast where curiosity meets knowledge?

THE NO-MOVE MOVE

Neither one of us knew who came up with it first.
It was a joint innovation,
a product of our brilliant conversations.
We'd share the prizes.

We liked the sense of continuity
with mathematics and with life.
It reminded us of the invention of zero,
the wisdom of sitting tight.

I don't recall how many games
of Our Chess we played
(hardly minding which of us won)
before we came unstuck

when I followed your No-Move with my own
and then we No-Moved back and forth
until we set each other off.
We thought we'd never stop laughing.

MATHS TEACHER

He pauses after every line
to name the principle
that warrants the next,
then speaks just what he is writing,
lifting his voice
above the click and scratch of chalk.

We watch the derivation unfold
beyond his shoulder,
copy it into our exercise books.

His pitch is a notch higher,
his scribble a smidgeon quicker
as we approach the conclusion
together, him stooping
to the lower quadrant of the board,
us craning our necks, thumbing a page,

and now a drum-roll
as he slides the boards,
stands tall again.

The final equation.
A triple underline
before he turns,
straightens down his smile.
A small throw of the chalk from hand to hand.

He checks his watch. *Five minutes left.*
Anything you'd like me to run through, quickly?

Yes, sir. The door.

Dear Mr Harrison,
Some thirty-five years on
and now, I learn, six months too late,
I offer this apology.

PLATO

A man stands in front of a life-size statue of a fox terrier
sitting up with its head cocked to one side, interested
but patient. The man's head is also tilted a little
and he is himself statue-still, feet spread for stability
while behind him his wife dips into the backpack he's wearing,
a blue-grey canvas day-bag with leather fastenings.
She has already taken a guidebook from an interior pocket
and is using the opportunity, the book gripped under her chin,
to do some rearranging, better to support their evolving plan for the day,
updated predictions about the coastal weather.
And so the bright cagoules emerge like a magician's scarves
before being refolded and squeezed deeper.
The sandwich box is stirred toward the surface.

This is what Plato meant by division of labour.
Every state must have a farmer, a builder, a weaver and a shoemaker,
and every marriage needs a packer and a carrier,
one who knows where things are when the other asks for them.

The man's gaze drops to the lengthy inscription on the plinth
and when she comes alongside, he summarises, pointing to sentences
from which she draws her own remindings, adds some names
he has forgotten,
and stitches them into the dog's story, which is the story of a local doctor,
now part of the couple's story too. As they turn to continue their walk,
she reaches for the dog's head and fondles its metal ears.

DESIGN AND TEST

A high whine irritates the air
where two planes fly.
As one, they dive, curve north, then climb again,
seeming more distant than they are,
real against the empty sky.

Ankle-deep in clover,
the friends stand close, the way they've stood
for half their lives.
Each holds a box, his thumb on a lever.
They squint toward the bright beyond the wood.

Men at play. A game in which the stake
is every careful pencil line
of winter's garage evenings,
measuring and making cuts in plastic.
Today's the test of their design

and care, those nights worked late
to the oil stove's knock and burn,
when what fed them was an image—
this dazzling blue-green light,
that long banked turn.

FLY FLYING

A house-fly woozily browses the economy cabin
miles above the Atlantic

and somewhere a mouse is scurrying out of a cargo ship
and nosing deeper into the dock,

a virus is crossing the bridge of a kiss
made urgent after a long separation

and a joke is being told in a new language,
half a world from where it was invented.

The fly twists onto the plane's plastic ceiling,
reeled in by a reading light.

It tiptoes the injection-moulded contours
of an overhead locker, upside down

and somewhere a child is wondering
whether a moth can fly through rain,

and does a birdcage weigh less when the bird is flying,
assuming there is room to fly.

STATISTICAL INFERENCE

I've heard it said more people are alive
than dead. Wrong. Since the species got its start,
one hundred and five billion have died;
just seven billion survive and some of those
at imminent risk of being reclassified,
like us lot, six miles high.
How many people are in the sky?

Let's count books. A nine-figure number
but not enough to go round,
and loads that have never seen action,
flicked through once and abandoned,
lying in heaps beside the bed.
What's the fraction currently being read?
Is that like people alive or people flying?

Either way, it can't be especially improbable
a person right now is in the clouds
with a novel. Something about this one though,
who leans over her blanketed lap,
who turns a page, then pushes her hair
behind one ear, so engrossed
she seems not to notice the turbulence.

PEELING A TANGERINE FOR MADELEINE

Pierce the skin
in a single place,
feel the acid sting
beneath the finger nail,
breathe the citrus spray.

Tease the peel from the flesh.
Stretch the web
of spittle-like pith
until it relents

but be gentle,
just the one spiral tear
so that when the flesh
is divided then served
the skin is spared

and reverts to its proper shape.
Nearly a sphere,
a miniature planet
with a giant San Andreas fault.
The Joke Tangerine,
a shell with no yolk,
the sac without a heart.

The heart is with Madeleine,
who is devouring it
segment by segment.

ANGER MANAGEMENT AT THE OPEN DAY

The Snake-Oil Crisis
is what the Head of Economics
called his talk about short selling and the credit crunch,
which kept me from hearing very much at all
about Religious Studies
or appreciating the vaunted common room.

And now the labs,
where a pleasingly stereotypical scientist
measures liquids into a flask
and whisks the resulting solution to a vortex.
Its colour darkens through amber to metal blue,
then oscillates between the two.
It's beautiful and mystifying
but I'm angry again
about my children's futures,
people selling what they never owned.

When I tune back in, we've all marched on
to the Mathematics classroom,
where the teacher's claiming that
market forces, chemical reactions,
it's all the same to her equations. Eco-systems too:
a lot of rabbits means more foxes
means fewer rabbits means fewer foxes means
a lot of rabbits, she says (I paraphrase).

She draws a pair of sine waves on the board.
Outside somewhere, rabbits sniff the breeze,
sleek red foxes are licking their lips and paws.

THE SCIENTIFIC METHOD

Maddy and I sit reading on the couch,
comfy in our silence, when she asks me
if I've noticed the way grown-up books
print the author's name bigger than the title
but books for kids have things the other way round.

I haven't, and once we've checked
against her Jacqueline Wilson, my Paul Auster,
we go to the front room together.

You're a scientist!, I say, as we sample
at random from the shelves of paperbacks,
one after another lending support
to the first half of her hypothesis,
and I'm your Research Assistant.

We hurry upstairs to her bedroom
and start to inspect her old picture books.
I pause sometimes to look inside, wanting
once more to read a few pages out loud
and point to the brightly painted happenings
but Maddy is an insistent inquirer, driven
by the accumulation of evidence
convincing us both she's onto something.

Only when we move to the newer books
do we meet our first exception:
Roald Dahl is bigger than the BFG.
Although not as friendly, I say
and we laugh, but I notice her deflate a little.

I tell her it doesn't matter, nothing
about human behaviour is neat and tidy.
When people say, say... *girls read more than boys,*
they don't mean all girls read more than all boys.
What matters is the tendency, the pattern
beyond chance, which calls for an explanation.

She's almost convinced, and I stop at that,
keep for a later day my thoughts about the exceptions
helping to find the best theory,
and how this is my favourite part of the process,
when the phenomenon itself is shifting
in the light of data and dialogue,
and the work—the fun—is still beginning.

CHICKEN QUESTIONS

Why the chicken?
And who to credit, or blame?

Philosophers reaching for poetry?
Did they guess their rhetorical coinages
would outlive their names?

In any case, since Darwin,
the one about the egg can be answered.

As every question must have a first asker,
so every species has a first member,
a standard bearer in the big parade of Life.

And because a bird's genotype is fixed
when the egg is fertilised,
the original chicken must have hatched
from a chicken egg. Therefore,
the egg came first!

But how did the parents respond
to a baby so new and so special?

Did they nurture it,
love-blind to its idiosyncrasies?

When it matured, how did it find a mate?

Did it search far and wide,
crossing road after road,
turning its bobbing, scarlet-combed head
this way, then that?

If it failed, could we really call it the first chicken?

In desperation, did it fly
but pathetically, like a birdman from a pier,
wanting to be something it wasn't?

INSIGHT

An owl closes its eyes
before the instant of connection
with the vole.

A camera showed us,
which opens its own eye
only for the tiniest fraction of a second,

a camera most likely designed
by a man in half-moon glasses
who pores over an engineering drawing

then rocks back from his desk
on the rear legs of his steel-framed chair
and closes his eyes.

WORD

❃

'A person who knows a word knows much more than its meaning and pronunciation.'

Miller, G. A. (1999). On knowing a word.
Annual Review of Psychology, 50(1), 1-19.

LANGUAGE AND THOUGHT

On my left, the stack of unread exam scripts.
On my right, the stack of those I've marked,
which contains no scripts at all. Perhaps only
a certain kind of academic would call it a stack,
though everyone has dealings with the empty set,
the set of things described and held in mind
but which do not exist—shirked chores
that dispatch themselves, perfect answers
to open questions, whatever we long for or miss.
The paper stack returns my stare. Child-like,
it grows a few inches taller every year.

DYSLEXIA

A hard thing to explain to an eight-year-old.
How to lift from everything we know
a clutch of truths by which he'll be consoled.
I keep to what it doesn't mean, name
the famous cases. Hard to answer no
when he asks quietly, *Are you the same?*

MIMESIS

Buffalo buffalo Buffalo buffalo buffalo buffalo Buffalo buffalo.

But nobody had seen it happen
until this traveller—
linguist, philosopher—

pulled off the road
on the long drive
from Brooklyn to Niagara,

a winter field, white page
where heavy glyphs
shove and shoulder,

puffs of snow at their hooves,
steam at their flanks
and from noses
which snort their own name,

and tough to know
which of the herd
impose their will
on which of the others,

who follows who
in the ebb and flow
where the bullied bully

and they all huff and shuffle
together, apart, together,
blur almost into a single creature,
one idea.

OPENING THE DICTIONARY

Your indigo blouse hangs in the wardrobe,
a dictionary of idioms
waiting for gesture and breath.

Even as you dress,
it starts to speak
in shimmering creases and flows.

Its ad-libbed script
is a play with the window-light,
later, a rhyme for the winter sun.

Lastly, a show by the fire:
the silk-fall from your shoulders,
the ink-blot at your ankles on the hardwood floor.

LOVER

A pullover against the frost,
a glove re-paired,
golden plover on the blanket bog,
sweet clover in the common,
coral over the coastal shelf,
a halo very jauntily drawn

above a stick-figure man.

SEAHORSE

Hippocampus, it's obvious
why you were given your name
but I would prefer Sea Knight,
after the chess piece.

The horse/hippo business
draws altogether
too much attention
to your lack of substance.

No wonder you seem self-conscious,
always turning
your best side to the camera.
Who would even know you

otherwise than in profile,
that defiant snout and your tiny tail's
counterintuitive spiral?
From the front, you must be nothing

but eyes on a gnarled stick, eyes wide
with the glamour of sharp-edged coral.
And your orientation's all wrong,
especially for a fish; it offers you

to the mercy of local currents,
the ocean's moods and whims.
Take care, Sea Knight, as you make
your wonky way across this treacherous game.

GIVEN NAME

Too many in my year at school and one
I couldn't stand. Too readily misspelled.
Of course, I learned to live with it, going by
the short form she preferred not to use.
But only since it started to slip her mind
have I held close this common given name:
imagining her sounding it against
alternatives, respecting her concern
to mark the equal bloodline from her father,
and hearing in it the voice of the young woman
who called me from my sleep those school-day mornings.

IN THE FLOATING TEMPLE

Spring, Summer, Fall, Winter ... and Spring (film)
Kim Ki-Duk (2003)

Between the mattresses
where the master and his pupil sleep
there is no dividing wall
but in the wall that isn't there
there is a doorframe and a door.

Listen to the click of the latch.
It is the lake's lapping at the shore
that lets you hear the quiet of the forest.

The arc on the hinge
is the friends' shared glance
that speaks across a hall.

The draught by the jamb
is the sip of water
from the explorer's flask.

The grain in the bamboo
is the letter from abroad,
the love poem in a drawer.

The doorway is the master's knowledge
and the pupil's calling.

COLLABORATION

A nursery assistant drops a clothes peg.
A toddler bustles over to pick it up and hand it back.
Forget what the politicians say about competition.
Forget the dog-eat-dog of TV nature programmes,
the open-mouthed parasite on the fish's tongue.
Walk down a busy pavement and count your collisions.
Look at the supermarket, where foragers form orderly queues,
or the office, the assembly line,
everyone building on another's contribution.
All conversation works this way.
Meanings dance into existence with a lean and sway
of gestures and facial expressions, pardons and *uh-huhs*—
a dance so balanced we barely notice, until I finish one of your
sentences. Even our quarrels are a joint production,
each of us helping the other to say those things.

LOANWORD

Neither of us has much French
but I step back while you take charge
and as I watch I could believe
you were the teacher, setting questions

and nodding when your student—
the delicatessen assistant—points to the correct answer.
I begin to suspect the meal is being chosen
with the test in mind,

so many items with names that our tongue
has borrowed from hers: baguettes,
pâté, les pains au chocolat. *Pique-nique,*
you smile, to explain the principle of the lesson.

Three hours down the road,
we lock our bicycles together
and spread a tablecloth on the grass
beside a slow, brown river.

While I pour the Perrier
you busy yourself with a penknife
and place the first sandwich
in front of me: *Voilà!*

Another loanword, and this one
sounds perfect on your voice,
announcing an everyday gift
with its modest Hey Presto.

TRANSLATING THE PROVERB

The Japanese say
Not seeing is a flower.
But don't look away

from whatever scene
draws your gaze. Don't close your eyes.
That's not what they mean.

Not quite. The saying's
point is that it's possible
to overthink things.

Some propositions
can't be proved: the better truths
are intuition's.

And if I've somehow
always known this, still I learned
it again just now,

escaping the glare
of information to breathe
some chilly March air,

when it came to me
where the path to the field turns
past the cherry tree.

SECONDHAND

A chanced-upon shop in a strange town
but I've been here before. Yes, there's a bell
jangling as I close the door behind me,
nod *hello* to the bookseller.

I warm to my task by sampling a shelf
I'm unaware of choosing—
perhaps light from the window
picked out a triangle of dust, a signpost;
perhaps the colours of certain spines combined
to capture my attention.

I'm celebrating what's haphazard and accidental,
hoping to be taken by something
unfamiliar, charmed by a surface,
or else to recognise what I can no longer retrieve,
an old note to myself, buried in the stack.

Here are the pleasures of a ritual
that allows variation, the scent
of each opened book's breath,
the satisfaction simply in being reminded

and further, the way a find can trigger a search, re-search:
that unravelling and mapping of the mind's network
onto the geometry of the display.

I'll enjoy deferring a while
my hunt for the few titles
I always look for, almost hopelessly

and mystify myself
by taking a sharpened interest
in books I already own.
How glad I am to find one, to ease it free
and page through its front matter
checking for inscriptions.

LITTLE SOLDIER

What was Stuart's mum thinking of,
sending him to school wearing long trousers,
the rest of us all in shorts?

This comes to me now, as I pay for my chops
and notice a cartoon on the butcher's wall
of a piglet, rosy-cheeked, stepping out in style.

I picture Mrs Pig, kissing her little soldier goodbye
the morning he leaves for market
in his stripy pinafore, a pork pie hat.

MIND

❋

'If the organism carries a 'small-scale model' of external reality and of its own possible actions within its head, it is able to try out various alternatives, conclude which is the best of them, react to future situations before they arise, utilise the knowledge of past events in dealing with the present and future, and in every way to react in a much fuller, safer and more competent manner to the emergencies which face it.'

Craik, K.J.W. (1943). *The nature of explanation.*
Cambridge: Cambridge University Press.

GUESSING GAME

He'd been surprised to find it in his coat pocket on the way to work—
a small plastic chicken from Old MacDonald's Farm.

That lunchtime he managed to sit beside her in the cafeteria.
He asked her to close her eyes and hold out a hand,
missed a beat as she complied.

He placed the chicken on her palm, *What's this?*
Get it right and you can keep it.

She made a fist, unclenched it again.
She cupped the toy in her two hands,
shook it like a die.

She took it in her fingertips, turned it, touched it,
all the time her eyes closed, her tongue just showing.
It feels like a chicken.

As she opened her eyes, he was already wondering
how he'd explain to his daughter.

PERSONAL IDENTIFICATION NUMBER

It must stay
minded but mine's
clever the way

it combines
a Mersenne prime
with my first home

so any time
it won't come
I have a cue:

can't be divided,
can't be returned to
uninvited.

BITE

Dawn is whitening the shutters
and I take cover beneath the sheets
too late. It's right where a nurse
would hold her finger to check my pulse.
Scratching is asking for trouble
and not-thinking is unthinkable
so I think hard about the itch
trying to push it to the edge
of my self—with the mosquito
that made it, now whining, now quiet,
out to that hotter summer
we camped near Buttermere,
Richard at the lake, framed by the scarp,
his naked back a moonscape.
None of us were with the one
we'd marry. Nobody had lost a son.
Richard bends to splash his shoulders
and yells out at how cold it is.

THE KINDS OF STRANGER

There's the stranger you find yourself following
down an empty street.
You bend to tie a shoelace
or hurry past on the other side.

There's the one with whom you share
a late-night taxi from the airport,
the snow heaped on the verges,
the driver oblivious to risk
asking, as you reach the city,
whose hotel to visit first.

There's the needy stranger
in the cold waiting room,
eyes locked onto yours.
When you hide in your paperback
he asks what you're reading.

And there's the stranger you pass
in the snicket on your way to the post office,
the one you notice again
when you return your library books
and who later notices you
fiddling a coin into a trolley
at the supermarket.
Your shy nods open over weeks
into a liaison of full-blown hellos—
you and this stranger
about whom you know only
that smile, the paths you both walk
and everywhere they might lead.

CANOEIST

Your gaze patrols the water and your pull
is long. Night's rains have made the river full.

Now that the surface-ruffling wind has died,
you see the hawthorn flow, the alders glide.

Beside the boat, your blade cuts through the sky,
uncovering the stars the clouds imply.

BAD HOTEL

'Every poet has a bad hotel poem'
Robin Robertson

It seemed promising and yes,
accommodating, the stooped hotelier
leading me up the stairs with two keys,
so as to offer me a choice.
He explained, as he unlocked the first room
that it was the bigger and the brighter,
newly decorated and enjoyed a park view
but had a wasps' nest in the bathroom.

A better man than me would have taken it,
thrown caution through the picture window
in the name of light and life: to bathe
in the glow of that layered, papery bulb,
to inspect its scalloped surface,
the spit and polish of a thousand fastidious limbs,
and to attend its low music, naked,
toothbrush in hand.

GIRL ON THE STAIRS

The morning you had the test which revealed
the sex of our second child, sibling for Joel,
you chose not to phone but to drive unannounced
from the hospital to the campus, where you climbed
the stairs—in your state!—to my sixth floor office
and ran into me somewhere around the fourth
rushing down to lecture with my head so full
of the General Problem Solver that when I unfolded
the scrap of paper pressed into my palm
as if it delivered secret instructions,
a password, or my role in a guessing game,
and read the single hand-written word *Girl*
I barely managed to return your smile
and to give you the quickest of kisses before
hurrying off, reluctant even to recollect
the encounter.

Eighteen years on,
the four of us together again for the weekend,
talking sexual politics at the kitchen table,
I can enjoy almost everything about it:
the stairwell with its echoes of unseen footsteps,
tall window edging you with a dazzle of white
Cardiff sky, the crinkled message in my fingers
and your breathless, uncrushable delight.

FEATURE

The cinema crowd exits the Little Theatre
and enters a city darkened by new rain.
They blink at the mannequins
in the shop window opposite before turning
toward the Cross Bath's stubby portico
or else the alley beside The Grapes.

A woman in raincoat and headscarf is hurrying,
face dipped to the shining wet flagstones,
dragging a broken double behind her, part reflection,
part shadow. She's rushing for a bus
and away from something in someone else's life.
Passing a streetlight, she overtakes herself.

A young couple lean on each other as they walk.
They have learned another half-truth about love
and about their own love, learned how lucky they are
to face an uncertain future. They separate
to step either side of a puddle,
then reach out their hands like dancers.

EQUINOX

The tilted planet's spin and arc
finding a balance between light and dark—
between the loud and silent park—
betrays a mind so geared to means and ends
that all experience depends
on past comparisons and future trends.

In March we seize the eager day,
a morning vigorously underway,
an evening reaching out for May.
Whereas September is a night begun
too soon, a night which won't be done
until we see the far side of the sun.

IMP OF THE PERVERSE

Heels on the yellow line, you eye the track.
Of course it won't happen, although the tug
feels ineluctable. You don't step back
but shrink deeper inside your coat, part shrug,
part flinch. A small step for a body, ergo
it comes to mind. All you can do is make
some promises, hug last night's warmth, and argue
your way through. Suppose free will is fake.
Darwinian selection couldn't tend—
surely?—toward a trigger-happy brain
which, loaded with your experience, would end
things just because it sees how. Then again,
what kind of brain is mustering this doubt?
In a moment, the train will find it out.

INFARCT

It's plain, yet strange to realise
that every item of the mind
must breathe in order to survive.

When oxygen is compromised
an idea can expire,
like a canary in a mine.

Here at the pithead of your eyes,
where darkness spills out into light,
I'm leaning, listening for signs—
birdsong, the drum of caged flight.

THE KNOWLEDGE

Kings Cross. A line of taxis.
I walk past toward the trains,
envying the idling cabbies
their peculiarly adapted brains.
Hippocampus after hippocampus
swollen with the knowledge it remembers.

Not that you'd guess, seeing them doze.
Perhaps what happens is a kind
of compensation by the mind:
the hippocampus grows
at the expense
of some neglected competence

and my own knack for getting lost implies
a hippocampus under-size
together with a surfeit
somewhere else—I'd bet
whatever bit
remembers things I'm trying to forget.

Easier to be a taxi driver,
letting things go
the better to know
the roads on both sides of the river.
Taking a kerb-side nap
with all the memories folded like a map.

SOIL

It's here, but hidden.
It stains the clothes of the first workers,
the kneeling children
who poured the street from their hot buckets.
It's the tattered strain
of what's been forgotten. It loiters
deep in the town's brain,
under concrete, clinging to moisture.
It's waiting for cracks
in the car parks and the factories,
for seeds of wild grass
recalled on the breeze.

MEME

I'm waiting for an opening sentence,
something to ease myself into the lecture
as much as the still-chattering students.
The woman on the front row's face is a picture.
Who does it remind me of? It's my sister,
right before I delivered the eulogy
at the funeral. I quickly look past her,
then make busy with the technology
of smudged touchscreen, pernickety projector
and start to blather, just to be moving.
Sure enough, after a minute the lecture
is carrying me, sometimes unnerving
me with something I hear myself remark,
and always the struggle to limit digressions,
steering the train back to the rough track
of my slides. I'm considering questions
about the content, rather than the structure,
of thought. My students, au fait with internet jargon,
perk up to hear of Dawkins' coinage, reduction
of 'mimeme', blend of memory and gene.
A meme is an idea, I say, *which spreads*
across its human hosts—a replicator,
such as wearing a baseball cap backwards...
But when I try to generate more,
the tradition of eulogizing the dead
jumps out and ambushes my mind.
Ideas have schemes of their own is what gets said
while this one hunts for another to hide behind.

TIME

❄

'Since memory traces are, we believe, in large part static and persist simultaneously, it must be assumed that they are spatially differentiated. Nevertheless, reproductive memory appears almost invariably as a temporal sequence, either as a succession of words or acts. [...] Spatial and temporal order thus appear to be almost completely interchangeable in cerebral action.'

Lashley, K.S. (1951). The problem of serial order in behavior.
In L. A. Jeffress (Ed.), *Cerebral mechanisms in behavior.*
New York: Wiley.

SPACE-TIME

As soon as we'd helped each other pitch our tents
we headed down to the water to hire boats,
rowed out to the centre of the lake
and let the boats drift, close enough to talk.
Skirting the exams just done, we stayed in a future
which Jeremy called our 'diaspora'.
Was it the conversation or the current
made us late, cost the next hour's rent?
Back at camp, we cracked open beers
and carried on till the sun gave way to stars.
We searched the sky for impromptu constellations
honouring our surrounds, the Stove, the Fence,
then Jeremy, always so serious,
we never knew how sad, picked out Polaris
and showed us how to use the Plough to find it.
On a roll, he recounted
how Trobriand islanders navigate
the scattered archipelago at night.
They think of their canoe as stationary
while the islands move, those ahead drifting nearer,
those astern sliding ever farther away.
At the start of each leg of the journey
they point the canoe's bow like a needle
toward a mark on the horizon's dial
(a mark defined by stars rising or setting)
and pull. I remember Jeremy repeating
something about space-time equivalence,
the rest of us staring at our hands.

A LIFE IN THE DAY

Strolling alongside the massive hospital, I'm convinced.
There are so many people in this city
that someone here today is my exact age
on every day of my life.

Begin with a newborn in the maternity wing
and roll out a life, one person at a time,
from crib to crib, away in a car,
through the crumbling schools
and polished banks, the side-street garages,
through the high ceilinged apartments
with their shuttered windows and antediluvian plumbing.

A strange life to lead—
though offering its own attractions—
new families and homes, not to mention selves,
a catholic education
and then, small wonder, finding it difficult to settle,
dropping out of college, trying on careers
like cardigans, tasting wives like wines.

And the eighteen-thousand-three-hundred-and-sixth day?
Well—that might as well be mine, a seer
of sights with a train ticket in my jacket pocket,
a calculator open on my smartphone,
smiling at a woman who smiles back as she passes,

and remembering an earlier Saturday
when I was this boy on a bicycle
freewheeling to his weekend job

as well as looking forward, as I reach the park,
to playing cards with my oldest friend
on the table near the railings, playing
until the chestnut tree's shadow
covers our game.

SUNDIAL

Surely it's not right . . .
though it shows a brave face,
that plump-cheeked, gaudy Sun.

Portalled back to the fifteenth century,
I could no more help with its design
than I could hurry its being supplanted
by a mechanical timepiece.

An engineering process involving
both kinds of compass
would defeat my skills.

And if I could explain longitude,
the way solar time varies across its stripe,
what would the townspeople care?

It's not as though they ever rubbed their eyes
in the square thinking, *That must be fast.*

The tailor, the smith, the chandler, the clerk worked
to the same shadow, and local affairs
ran like clockwork.

Only a rare visitor,
pressed for time and tired beyond mention,
was perplexed by how much he'd lost
on his passage over the mountain.

‘GLENN GOULD INTO THE MUSIC’

Photograph by Yousuf Karsh, 1957

He stares at the keys beyond his hands.
Not a note is depressed or even touched.

He is listening to the chord just played,
already hearing the ones to come,

just as his hands, high and arched,
hold traces of both past and future

whether they are rising or falling
or in that moment’s stillness between.

There is no blur, although perhaps
the tips of his fingers soften

into their reflections on the polished wood,
the way sound softens into quiet.

WATCH

In my parents' wardrobe
a fortnight before Christmas, I found
perfection: a diver's watch with a black dial,
luminous baton markers and hands,
and a ratcheted bezel, so time could be made
to begin again with a simple twist.

Nights I would load the phosphor from my angle-poise,
then lie awake just to watch
the second hand sweep the dark like radar.

I think about it now in some landfill, face covered, still.
And suddenly remember its predecessor,
a child's watch, so hurriedly discarded,
on which Hopalong Cassidy, cowboy philosopher,
lassoed the minute, fired his pistol at the hour.

CHRONOLOGY OF THE HEART IN TWO AND A HALF RHYMES

In the fourth century BC, Aristotle declared it the seat
of reason and the source of body heat.

Galen (circa 200 AD) described it as hard.
Hard meat,
hard working, hard to hurt.

Leonardo, around 1490, made an art
of sketching it on his worksheet.

In the 1600s, William Harvey contrived to chart
the circulation of blood. He called the heart
'the principal part'
but wasn't the first to compare it
to a pump. That was Descartes.

Twentieth-century science discovered the 'heart-
brain' (Armour, 1991), which messages *medulla oblongata*,
the brainstem-half with functions first remarked
by Freud. Back to the start,
circle complete, a neurocardiological repeat
of Aristotle's thinking heart.

Like so many, the old, the ill-starred,
Jim's heart
was his defeat
(2008). His multi-infarct
dementia was caused by an irregular beat.

TARDIS

'DR WHO VISITS PENARTH'
Penarth Times, March 2008

After our row that early July morning
I walked through to the back bedroom
with my coffee and my cereal
and looked down across our unkempt garden
to the neighbours': shocking in white.
Their perfect lawn and apple tree,
the prissy wooden summer house,
the stone dividing wall
midwintered by inches of snow.
Soon the film crew appeared
with their cameras and cables,
setting and angling a pair of spotlights
onto a scene whose sheer weirdness
remained untouched by the explanation.
I recognised the current Doctor
and watched a member of the crew dispose
the Time Lord and the girl like toy soldiers.
I stayed watching as a brief unheard conversation
was played again and again.
I once had a friend whose backpack we called The Tardis.
If someone asked for a map or a bottle opener—
there's one in here somewhere—
emptying sweaters and torches onto the ground by his feet.
What impressed me most was how he managed
to get everything back in. If I so much as unfold
a map, I can never seem to make it right again.
I might as well try to put snow back
inside a cloud, or any other snow machine.

HALF A LIFETIME

From morning they walked east
along the towpath. Direction
was their only plan; all destinations
local and impromptu, the places
they found themselves.
Their conversation became the canal,
connecting neighbourhoods
by other than the usual arc,
threading railway-like between
the romantic and the all-too-real:
the undecorated backs of homes
and factories, graffiti promises.
There were pigeons under the bridges
and outside an aviary in the zoo
where a small gang flaunted
its feral freedom
to the ibises and egrets.
They walked alongside houseboats
full of different lives
(as well as one full of books
they folded their tall
bodies down into).
Every time they checked their watches
they'd lost an hour
so that over the course of the day
they lost one more whole day,
which they resolved to win back,
although a teaspoonful
compared with half a lifetime.

TO: LINDA

'Last night you went to Shropshire on the train
and saw everything. Darling, don't explain.'
Linda Chase (11 July 1941 – 8 April 2011)

You used to send them by email
even during those six months
when I was your lodger.

Poems from a teacher to her student
so buoyed by the compliment
as to dare comment.

Poems that I kept safe, saved
along with your messages,
which are poems too.

Your laugh comes and goes as I read
until I find the only poem
you were shy to show me.

You worried I'd be embarrassed
that you appeared to have written
a sonnet for me

about my commute from South Wales
during a week of heavy snow.
And that you called me *Darling*.

You said the lines had come to you
as you searched for an open ending
and had felt perfect.

I replied that yes they were
and that nobody would ever know.
Darling, let them.

MODEL

Two miles along the towpath, kicking leaves,
I walked your poems to the bench at Bath
Top Lock. There, through the cloud of my own breath,
I turned the pages with my woolly gloves
and read, and read, until a crewman shouted
from a narrowboat heading downstream.
Would he reach the river before the storm?
Surprised, I checked the sky and said, *I doubt it.*

In five minutes, it starts to bucket down.
In ten, I'm dripping on the pub's stone floor
while peeling poems. Once they're freed, I stand
your book beside my whisky, pages fanned,
and spread my hands in front of the open fire.
And then I notice what I've done.

AFTER THE TRAM CRASH

I came around in the ambulance, a mess
of wires and tubes, a press of paramedics
asking questions I couldn't understand.
In hospital, her visits were the high spots
of anyway untroubled days—long sleep
and something close to sleep but even better.
I wasn't at all upset when the doctor asked
in a European accent, careful English,
Do you mind if I show you to my students?
You look rather peculiar at the moment.
But afterwards, asking him for a mirror,
I knew the kindness of her daily smiles.
My face was black and blue and red all over,
a traffic victim painted by a child.

My first night out, we went to see Paul Simon
at the Concertgebouw. We missed the last train home
and had to hitchhike back to Rotterdam,
so I pulled my scarf up high, my hat down low,
and let her thumb and beauty work the traffic.
Then later, making love, the rifle crack
of my left ulna breaking as I pulled
my body down the iron bed. Drugged numb,
I laughed it off as an accident waiting to happen
and slept beside her, leaving it till morning
to revisit A&E, not dreaming
that later the same winter I would lie
in that bed and cry, because I was alone,
or else because I was alive.

JOURNEY HOME

On every long journey home, there's such a place.
It can be just a roundabout or a slip-road,
perhaps a farmhouse gable, a stand of trees.

Always the same small shift as it's passed,
the journey in some way over before its end.

In company, the conversation changes pace.
Alone, the mind gives itself away,
clicking into calm, or else unease.

RIDERS ON THE STORM

By early afternoon
we're in the city of giant tombs. We watch
an old Parisienne, as if a child,
reaching out nervously to touch
the demon-angel guarding Oscar Wilde.
I embarrass us by whistling a tune
beside the plainer grave of Jim Morrison,
and laughing at a thing so odd, so off,
as 'Fred' Chopin—perhaps the stonemason
began by inscribing too big an F?
Another life cut short.
We share a shot
of cognac on the long walk back. You spread
the map to reconsider our agreed route;
I open my purchase from the bouquinistes
to look for Lowell's 'For the Union Dead'
but snag on 'Adam and Eve', thinking about
the conversations where what matters least
is what gets said...
at sundown on a shore,
with alabaster pebbles under our shoes,
the estuary's hush. We trade some news,
only to register we're here once more,
noting the lights of Weston Super Mare,
the tidal water's height against the pier.

PIER

Beyond the waterfront parade
of small concerns, it makes its stand.
The freshly painted balustrade
   puts on a brave display
above the suck and swell that's fanned
around stanchions, licking them away.

The understructure has a crust:
the flock effect of seagull shit,
a blanket rash of molluscs, rust
   on rivet-heads and screws.
Yet even here they pretty it
with fluted columns and curlicues.

Call it vain, think it risible
to dig in, for appearance sake,
against the irresistible;
   it's what I've come here for.
I'll walk the pier's full length and take
the air toward my father's shore.

Notes & Acknowledgements

p. 11 'The Science of the Artificial' is inspired by Dan Sperber [Sperber, D. (2007). Seedless grapes: nature and culture. In E. Margolis & S. Laurence (Eds.), *Creations of mind: theories of artifacts and their representation*. Oxford: OUP] but its title derives from the classic book by Herbert Simon.

p. 14 'The Fractal Library': see Mandelbrot, B.B. (1967). How long is the coast of Britain? Statistical self-similarity and fractional dimension. *Science*, 156 (3775), 636-638.

p. 28 'Insight': Roger Elkin read his poem 'At moments of kill, the barn-owl's eyes are closed' at Dawn Gorman's poetry night, Words & Ears, in Bradford on Avon, 2013.

p. 33 'Mimesis': 'Buffalo buffalo Buffalo buffalo buffalo buffalo Buffalo buffalo' is a grammatical sentence invented by William Rapaport, and perhaps independently by others.

p. 41 'Translating the Proverb' might not rhyme were it not for Richard Wilbur's poem 'Ecclesiastes 11.1'. It is informed by a conversation with Kyoko Murakami of the University of Copenhagen.

p. 56 'The Imp of the Perverse' is a short story by Edgar Allan Poe.

p. 69 'Chronology of the Heart in Two and a Half Rhymes' takes its historical facts from a variety of online sources but in particular, up to Harvey, from https://web.stanford.edu/class/history13.

p. 72 'To: Linda': The epigraph is drawn from 'Sometimes Snow' in Linda Chase's last book: *Not Many Love Poems* (Carcanet, 2011).

p. 77 'Riders on the Storm': 'Adam and Eve' is the second part of Robert Lowell's 'Between the Porch and the Altar', which appeared in *Lord Weary's Castle* (Harcourt Brace, 1946) and is reprinted in *Selected Poems* (Faber and Faber, 1965).

Some of the poems in this volume first appeared in: *Agenda* (online), *Butcher's Dog*, *Domestic Cherry*, *Envoi*, *Magma*, *New Walk*, *Poetry Nottingham*, *Prole*, *Seam*, *Smiths Knoll*, *Snakeskin*, *South*, *The Chimaera*, *The Dark Horse*, *The Interpreter's House*, *The North*, *The Poetry Review*, *The Rialto*, *The SHOp*, *Under the Radar*. Several were also included in *The Probabilities of Balance*, Smiths Knoll (2010).

Thanks to all my poetry friends and teachers, and special thanks to Michael Laskey and Joanna Cutts. There is no better place to discuss poems than around Michael's table.